STARS OF MYTHOLOGY

STARS OF ROMAN MYTHOLOGY

NANCY DICKMANN

Gareth Stevens PUBLISHING

**Please visit our website,
www.garethstevens.com.
For a free color catalog of all
our high-quality books, call
toll free 1-800-542-2595 or
fax 1-877-542-2596.**

Cataloging-in-Publication Data
Names: Dickmann, Nancy. | Lilly, Matt, illustrator.
Title: Stars of Roman mythology /
by Nancy Dickmann, illustrated by Matt Lilly.
Description: Buffalo, NY : Gareth Stevens Publishing, 2026. |
Series: Stars of mythology | Includes glossary and index.
Identifiers: ISBN 9781482473360 (pbk.) | ISBN 9781482473377
(library bound) | ISBN 9781482473384 (ebook)
Subjects: LCSH: Mythology, Roman--Juvenile literature. |
Gods, Roman--Juvenile literature. |
Goddesses, Roman--Juvenile literature.
Classification: LCC BL803.D524 2026 | DDC 292.1'3--dc23

Published in 2026 by
Gareth Stevens Publishing
2544 Clinton St.
Buffalo, NY 14224

First published in Great Britain in 2017
by The Watts Publishing Group

Credits
Series editor: Sarah Peutrill
Series design and illustrations: Matt Lilly
Cover designer: Cathryn Gilbert
Picture researcher: Diana Morris

Pic credits: abxyz/Dreamstime: 1tl, 26cl, 28tc. Alexey Belov/ Dreamstime: 6-7 bg, 9tbg. Chandos/Shutterstock: 4c. Chronicle/ Alamy: 2b, 27c, 28bl, 28tr. Pablo Debat/Shutterstock: 27bg. Empire331/Dreamstime: front cover cr, 22c, 24br, 25cr. Fotoeye75/Dreamstime: 18c, 19c, 21t. http://www.freepik. com”>Designed by Freepik: front cover bg & b. Gors4730/ Dreamstime: front cover cl, 14c, 17b. Grubernst/CC Wikimedia: 12tr. Peter Horree/Alamy: 7c, 8br. Iakov Kalinin/Dreamstime: 18-19bg, 20bg, 21bg. Rafael Laguillo/Dreamstime: 12bl. Lasy/CC Wikimedia: 15c. Matt Lilly: 20b, 28tr. R.Nagy/Shutterstock: 13bg. Marie-Lan Nugyen/CC Wikimedia: 6c, 8bl, 9t. Phant/Shutterstock: 5c. Picturepoint/Topham: 5tl ,5tr, 10c, 11c, 13cl, 13cr. Elena Shchipkova/Dreamstime: 10-11 bg. Waters Museum, Baltimore/ CC Wikimedia: 16t. Tosca Weijers/Dreamstime: 23c, 24bl, 25cl.

Printed in the United States of America

CPSIA compliance information: Batch #CSGS26
For further information contact Gareth Stevens at 1-800-542-2595.

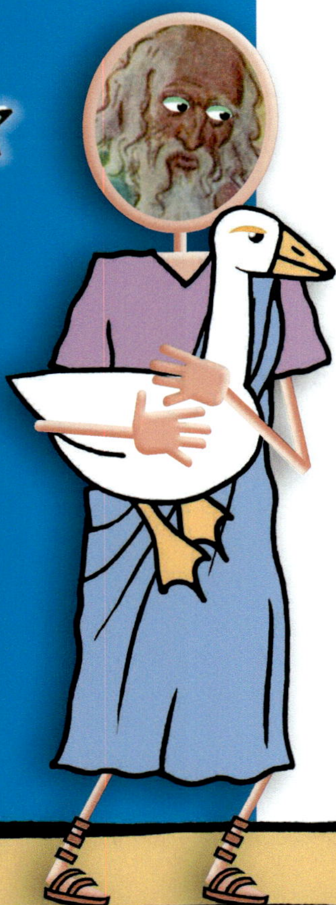

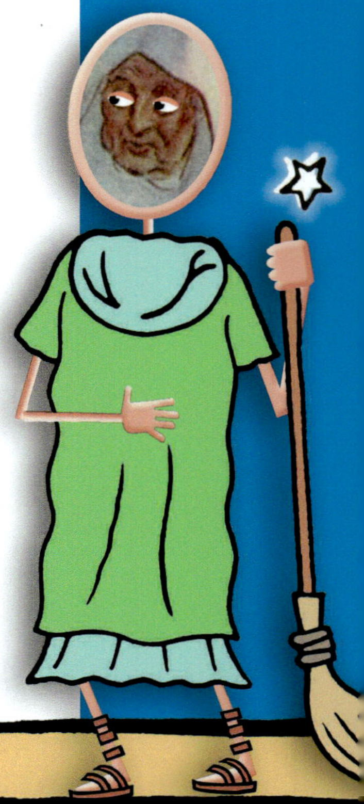

CONTENTS

ROMAN MYTHOLOGY

About two thousand years ago, the Romans ruled an enormous empire that surrounded the Mediterranean Sea and stretched as far north as Britain. The Romans were fierce soldiers as well as crafty politicians, skilled engineers, and well-traveled traders. Their influence can still be seen today in our architecture, language, and arts.

MYTHS AND LEGENDS

The Romans had a complicated religion, filled with gods, goddesses, heroes, monsters, and spirits. They believed that although the gods had supernatural powers, they were like humans in many ways: they fell in love and had children, and could feel hate and jealousy. The stories about the gods were a way of explaining the natural world and demonstrating how the ideal Roman was supposed to behave.

WORSHIPPING THE GODS

The Romans believed that gods and goddesses affected everyday life and therefore had to be kept happy. For example, Neptune was the god of the sea, so before a long voyage, a sailor would pray to Neptune and maybe sacrifice an animal as well. This was supposed to ensure that he had a safe journey. Romans prayed and offered sacrifices at their homes as well as in great temples.

ROMULUS

STORIES ABOUT ROME

Some Roman myths tell the story of how the city of Rome was founded and how it became powerful. Sometime around 19 BCE, the Roman poet Virgil wrote *The Aeneid*, which told how the hero Aeneas escaped from the Trojan War and came to Italy to found a new city called Lavinium. Aeneas was the ancestor of Romulus and Remus, the twin brothers who according to legend founded Rome.

REMUS

GODS WERE WORSHIPPED AT TEMPLES SUCH AS THE PANTHEON.

BORROWED STORIES

The Romans conquered many other peoples and often adopted the conquered peoples' myths and gods. For example, Aphrodite (the Greek goddess of love) was worshipped in Rome as Venus. The Roman god Jupiter has many similarities to both the Etruscan god Tinia and the Greek god Zeus. In many cases, the Romans adapted stories about other cultures' gods and goddesses to match the gods that they already worshipped.

DIDO AND AENEAS

READ THEIR STORY ON PAGES 8–9.

Fact file: DIDO

DIDO was from the city of Tyre, where her father was king. The king hoped that Dido and her brother, Pygmalion, would rule together after his death. But Pygmalion was ambitious and greedy, and he murdered Dido's husband, Sychaeus.

Afraid for her life, Dido fled to the northern coast of Africa. She struck a deal with the local ruler that he would sell her as much land as she could mark out with a bull's skin (hide). But clever Dido cut the hide into very thin strips, made them into a long string, and used them to mark out a huge area of land, which is where Carthage was built.

DIDO IN HER OWN WORDS:

VIEWS ON SIBLINGS:
My brother wins the prize for being awful. He murdered my husband for his money and took the throne for himself.

FAVORITE PLACE:
It's gotta be Carthage – the city is amazing! Pygmalion is welcome to keep Tyre for himself.

BIGGEST WEAKNESS:
When I fall in love, I fall hard. (Sometimes too hard, to be honest.)

SECOND BIGGEST WEAKNESS:
A tendency towards the dramatic.

Fact file: AENEAS

AENEAS was the son of Venus (the goddess of love) and the Trojan prince Anchises. He helped to defend Troy against the Greeks during the Trojan War. When the Greek attackers swarmed out of the Trojan horse to torch the city, Aeneas and a few other survivors escaped.

Aeneas believed it was his duty to found another great city for the Trojans. He embarked on a long sea voyage, with many adventures, before being shipwrecked on the African coast, near Carthage.

AENEAS IN HIS OWN WORDS:

THE PERKS OF BEING A DEMIGOD:
During the Trojan War, my mother came to the rescue more than once, and she got the other gods to help out too.

WHY I HATE THE GREEKS:
I lost nearly everything, including my wife, when they destroyed Troy.

I WOULD NEVER:
Break a promise, no matter what. Especially not if that promise was made to a god – I'm not stupid!

ALL FOR LOVE

Queen's suicide caps off tragic love story

Reports have reached us that Dido, Queen of Carthage, has died. Eyewitnesses saw her climbing onto a blazing pyre before stabbing herself, as the ships of the Trojan prince Aeneas sailed out of the harbor. Her death leaves her people reeling from the shock and asking themselves how it could all have gone so wrong.

Nearly a year ago, soon after Aeneas's arrival in Carthage, we interviewed Dido's sister, Anna, and at the time, she saw the newcomer as a gift from the gods. "Dido has been mourning her first husband for so long," she told us. "The attentions of a young Trojan hero might be just what she needs to move on."

And things did seem to be going well at first. The two soon fell in love and worked together to rule Carthage. But what went wrong?

A source at the palace told us that a few weeks ago, the prince was seen talking with a messenger who may have been the god Mercury. "Obviously, I've never met Mercury in person, so I can't be sure," said the source. "But who else wears winged sandals?" He went on to tell us that Mercury seemed to be reminding a reluctant Aeneas about a promise he had made to build a new city for the Trojans.

One of Dido's ladies-in-waiting provided the next clue. "I was passing the queen's chamber when I heard her arguing with Aeneas. Now, I would never eavesdrop, but I couldn't help overhearing. The prince was going on about something being his duty. Then Dido asked, 'Isn't love more important than duty?' And Aeneas didn't say anything – he just left . He nearly knocked me over as he stormed out. He looked wretched."

Then yesterday morning, the palace servants were ordered to take all of Aeneas's things out into the courtyard and burn them. "I thought it was Dido's revenge on him for having dumped her," a white-faced footman told us. "I could see Aeneas's ship setting sail. But then Dido rushed out and started climbing up the burning pyre. Before we could stop her, it was all over. She died for love."

ROMULUS AND REMUS

READ THEIR STORY ON PAGES 12–13.

Fact file: ROMULUS AND REMUS

According to Roman legend, the twins **ROMULUS** and **REMUS** were descended from Aeneas. Their mother, Rhea Silvia, was a priestess of Vesta, goddess of the hearth. Some versions of the story say that their father was Mars, the god of war.

It was against the law for the priestesses to have children. When the twins were born, the king ordered Rhea Silvia to be put in prison, and for the babies to be thrown into the River Tiber to die.

ROMULUS IN HIS OWN WORDS:

WHO'S THE DADDY?

No one really knows, but some people say that our father is the god Mars. That might be because we love fighting and arguing so much …

WORLD'S BEST EXCUSE:

If anyone complains about my manners or my behavior, all I have to say is, "What did you expect? I was raised by wolves!"

MY LEGACY:

This city I'm building is going to be the greatest ever. So of course I'm going to name it after myself. "Rome" has a nice ring to it, don't you think?

The servant who was supposed to throw the twins into the river couldn't bring himself to do it. To give them a chance at survival, he put them in a basket and watched them float away down the river.

The basket got caught in the roots of a fig tree, and a female wolf found the babies. She took them to her den, where she raised them alongside her own cubs. Eventually, the two boys were adopted by a kind shepherd called Faustulus.

REMUS IN HIS OWN WORDS:

A SHEPHERD'S LIFE:

Faustulus is a lovely guy, and I'm grateful to him for taking us in. But looking after sheep all day is 100 percent BORING.

BEST FRENEMIES:

My twin brother Romulus and I are inseparable. We get along … most of the time. But we also know how to push each other's buttons!

WHY I'M THE BEST TWIN:

At least I have a sense of humor – unlike Romulus. He just can't take a joke!

A SHEPHERD'S DIARY
BY FAUSTULUS

10TH DAY OF QUINTILIS:
Had the sheep out on the western hills today, and I found some babies. (Two boys, probably twins.) I'd gone looking for a she-wolf that had been killing my herd, and I found them with her. She was feeding them like they were her own cubs! Ah well, a wolf's mind works in mysterious ways. I'll take them home to my wife – she'll know what to do.

FAUSTULUS

A WEEK LATER:
The boys are settling in nicely, though I think living with wolves has affected their table manners! The wife's not pleased. We've named them Romulus and Remus.

SHE-WOLF

FIVE YEARS LATER:
I've started teaching the boys the art of being a shepherd. They bicker constantly and could even turn raising sheep into a competition! That's not such a bad idea, actually …

TEN YEARS LATER:
I always knew that Romulus and Remus's love of arguing would land them in trouble. They got into a fight with some other shepherds today, and Remus was arrested. Tomorrow I'll see if I can sort things out with the king.

The next day:

That Romulus is such a hothead! He got a bunch of his friends together and went to rescue Remus. I'm not looking forward to telling the wife that he killed the king in the process. Oops!

A few months later:

Those boys were never going to be satisfied with a shepherd's life. They've decided that this land isn't big enough to hold them and their egos, so they're going to build their own city.

The following week:

The boys took me to see the location they've chosen for their new city. Romulus wants to build on one hill, and Remus wants a different one. It's a stalemate!

21 April, 753 BCE:

A dark day. I went to see the boys; Romulus had started building his city. His wall was only waist high, so Remus started jumping over it, cracking jokes. Romulus got angrier and angrier, until he finally struck out and killed his own brother. I always knew their tempers would get them in trouble! As for me, I'll stick to sheep from now on.

JUNO AND VULCAN

READ THEIR STORY ON PAGES 16–17.

Fact file: JUNO

JUNO was the daughter of the god Saturn, and she eventually married her brother, Jupiter. The two of them reigned over all the other gods, and their children included Mars (god of war) and Vulcan (god of fire).

Jupiter was often unfaithful to her, but Juno had little time to waste being jealous. She was seen as a protector of Roman women and was the goddess of marriage as well as of childbirth. She traveled in a chariot pulled by peacocks.

JUNO IN HER OWN WORDS:

SHAMEFUL SECRET:
I know that you're not supposed to have a favorite child, but it's no contest between my two sons. Any mother would be proud of Mars – he's handsome and an amazing soldier. As for Vulcan, well… the less said, the better!

GUILTY PLEASURE:
I may have a teensy tiny thing for fabulous jewelry. But when you're the queen of the gods, you're expected to look good!

HOW TO KEEP ME HAPPY:
It's simple – let me get my own way.

Fact file: VULCAN

VULCAN was the son of Jupiter and Juno, but he was such an ugly baby that his mother rejected him, throwing him into the sea. One of his legs broke, leaving him with a permanent limp. He was raised by the sea-nymph Thetis in an underwater grotto.

Vulcan was fascinated by fire, and he soon became a skilled blacksmith. After he married Venus, the goddess of love, he set up a forge under Mount Etna in Sicily. Whenever Venus was unfaithful, his anger would make sparks and smoke erupt out of the mountain.

VULCAN IN HIS OWN WORDS:

MY PARENTS:
I guess that anyone who rules the entire world is bound to have high standards, so I was never good enough for Jupiter and Juno.

GREATEST ACHIEVEMENT:
Setting up a working forge under the sea. My stupid brother Mars wouldn't have had a clue how to do it, but they don't call me the god of fire for nothing!

WORDS TO LIVE BY:
Revenge is a dish best served cold.

THE GOLDEN THRONE

... JUNO'S STORY

I should have known that Vulcan would come back to haunt me one day. I just didn't know that it would be so uncomfortable!

I've tried and tried to get out of this stupid chair, but he knows his trade, I'll give him that. He must have wanted me to have a good think about how I've treated him over the years. And now he's got his wish.

Listen, any mother would have done the same as me, faced with a baby so ugly and deformed. There was no way a creature like that was living on Mount Olympus with the rest of us gods – I had no choice but to throw him into the sea.

How was I supposed to know that he'd be adopted by that sea-nymph Thetis? All these years and Thetis never said a word, until that day last week when I complimented her on her necklace.

It was a beautiful thing, made of gold and sapphires. I'd never seen anything so fine before and wanted one for myself. But Thetis immediately started looking shifty and wouldn't tell me where she'd gotten it.

I am nothing if not persistent (you have to be, as queen of the gods) so I kept pressing her. Finally, she admitted the truth. I couldn't believe it! That hideous little baby had grown up to be an incredibly talented blacksmith.

Of course, if he had divine skills then that changed everything. I told Thetis to send him to me, but a few days later, I got a message that he refused to come to see me. Me, his own mother!

He did send a throne, though, which was just as beautiful as the necklace – truly fit for a queen. I sat in it straightaway, but my weight triggered the trap, and metal bands sprang out to hold my wrists and ankles.

So I've been stuck here for three days now, getting more and more desperate. My husband Jupiter has sent a message to Vulcan, saying that he can have Venus, the goddess of love, as his bride if he'll only release me. I hope he agrees … I really need the bathroom!

CASTOR AND POLLUX

READ THEIR STORY ON PAGES 20–21.

Fact file: CASTOR

CASTOR'S mother was Leda, the queen of Sparta. She gave birth to four children at the same time – twin brothers Castor and Pollux and twin sisters Helen and Clytemnestra. It wasn't clear whether their father was Jupiter or her own husband, Tyndareus.

Castor grew up to be a skilled fighter. He was especially famous for his skill with horses. He and Pollux joined the crew of a ship called the *Argo* along with other famous heroes, helping Jason on his quest to find the Golden Fleece.

CASTOR IN HIS OWN WORDS:

FAVORITE HOBBY:
Give me a horse to ride, and I'm a happy guy. The wilder the better!

GREATEST ADVENTURE:
Too hard to choose. Hunting the Calydonian Boar, maybe, or rescuing my sister Helen after she was kidnapped.

I'M HAPPIEST WHEN:
Doing the hero thing. Sailing on the *Argo* was dangerous, but it was also great fun – lots of hanging out with the guys.

BEST FRIEND:
My twin brother Pollux – who else?

Fact file: POLLUX

Like his brother, **POLLUX** was a talented fighter. He was especially famous for his boxing skills and once killed a man with a single punch during a boxing match.

The two brothers were inseparable, traveling and having adventures throughout the ancient world. Although Castor and Pollux were identical twins, there was one key difference between them: Pollux was immortal, while Castor was not.

POLLUX IN HIS OWN WORDS:

FAMILY WEIRDNESS:
There's a rumor that Jupiter is my father, which is not so weird on its own, but the story is that he visited my mother in the form of a swan. Weird.

NOT MANY PEOPLE KNOW THIS:
I wasn't born like most people are – I hatched from an egg.

GREATEST TRIUMPH:
Flattening Amycus, King of the Bebryces, in a boxing match. He was the size of a mountain!

WHAT KEEPS ME AWAKE AT NIGHT:
I never want to be separated from my brother, but he's not immortal, and you know what that means …

FAMILY FEUD

The dust is still settling after the results of last week's speed-eating contest. Idas wiped the floor with his cousins, Castor and Pollux, but the conflict didn't end there...

It seemed like the perfect way to divide up the spoils of a cattle raid. The famous twin heroes, Castor and Pollux, had teamed up with their cousins, Idas and Lynceus, to steal a herd of cattle.

"They were arguing about how many cattle each should have," said a local shepherd who overheard the heated discussion. "Then Idas suggested that he cut an ox into four pieces. They'd each eat a piece, and whoever finished first would have first choice of the cattle."

Readers of these pages will know that only a fool would challenge the enormous Idas to an eating competition, but apparently Castor and Pollux didn't know that.

"Idas finished his piece in about two seconds flat," said the shepherd. "You should have seen him go! Then he snatched up Lynceus's portion and hoovered that up as well. Castor and Pollux had only taken a few bites when he grabbed their meat too."

The contest finished with Idas and Lynceus taking all the cattle, leaving the twins fuming … and plotting revenge.

Yesterday matters came to a head when Castor and Pollux stole back all the cattle, and their cousins raced over to get them back. "I saw it all go down," claims a local farmer's wife. "Idas and Lynceus came roaring over the hill, and Idas wounded Castor with his spear. Pollux saw what had happened and killed Lynceus with a single punch."

"The next thing I knew, a thunderbolt flew down from the sky and fried Idas. It must have been Jupiter – he's Pollux's dad, you know. Pollux was just standing there in shock. His two cousins were lying dead and his twin brother was bleeding to death at his feet. 'Jupiter, Jupiter!' I heard him cry as he dropped to his knees. 'Let me share my immortality with my brother!' Then there was this flash of light, and they were gone. But that night there was a new constellation in the sky: the twins."

The new constellation is called Gemini.

HERCULES AND ATLAS

READ THEIR STORY ON PAGES 24–25.

Fact file: HERCULES

HERCULES was the son of a god and of a mortal woman, Alcmene. Even as a baby he was incredibly strong, and he strangled a snake that came into his cradle to kill him. He was an expert fighter and chariot racer.

In a fit of madness, Hercules killed his wife and children. To atone for this, he agreed to complete 12 tasks for King Eurystheus of Mycenae. They included killing or capturing dangerous creatures, which would be impossible for most men.

HERCULES IN HIS OWN WORDS:

I DON'T LIKE TO BOAST, BUT ...
I'm stronger than anyone else I've ever met. Wanna arm-wrestle?

DIRTIEST JOB:
I had to clean out the Augean Stables. Thousands of cattle had been kept there for decades, without it having been cleaned once! That was totally gross.

CHECK MY STYLE:
My massive club and lionskin wrap show people that I mean business.

GREATEST WEAKNESS:
I don't like the word "weakness," but I am a bit short-tempered.

Fact file: ATLAS

ATLAS was one of the Titans, a race of early gods from Greek mythology. His parents were Iapetus and Clymene. With his parents and other family members, Atlas fought a mighty war against a younger generation of gods, the Olympians.

The Titans lost the war, and as a punishment, many of them were imprisoned in the deepest, darkest part of the Underworld. Atlas had a different punishment: he had to carry the weight of the heavens on his shoulders.

ATLAS IN HIS OWN WORDS:

KIDS THESE DAYS: Those Olympians think they're so great, with their thunderbolts and everything. They make me sick!

I'D BE UP FOR: Got a dangerous job that needs doing? Fighting monsters or whatever – I'm your man! Anything that doesn't involve carrying something heavy.

I COULD DO WITHOUT: Constant lower back pain.

TRICKED! ... ATLAS'S STORY

You think you've got it hard? Try holding the weight of the world on your shoulders … literally!

Long ago, I lost a war. Hey, it happens to the best of us, and my punishment was to carry the weight of the heavens, forever. And the skies aren't all fluffy clouds and twinkling stars either – they're HEAVY.

Now, everyone always asks how I could have been so thick as to be tricked by that poser Hercules. He had been assigned 12 tasks, and one of them was to collect some golden apples. They grow in the gardens of these nymphs called the Hesperides.

The gardens were guarded by a fierce dragon, and obviously Hercules didn't think he was up to the task, so he came to me. We quickly made a deal: he would hold the heavens for me while I got the apples. I cannot even begin to describe the relief of passing that heavy orb over to him and giving my impressive muscles a proper stretch.

The dragon was no match for me, obviously, and I collected the apples and started back. I took my time, though – it was so nice to just walk through that peaceful garden, carrying nothing heavier than a few golden apples.

In fact, I wondered, why take the heavens back at all? Why not just leave Hercules to hold them up?

You should have seen his face when I refused to take them back. It was priceless! But then he sighed and said, "All right, you win. But can you hold them for just a sec while I fold up my cloak to cushion the weight?"

My newfound freedom made me feel generous, so I graciously agreed. I put the apples down and Hercules passed the orb to me.

As soon as it was on my shoulders, he said, "You absolute fool, Atlas," as he picked up the apples. "Enjoy the rest of eternity!" And then he sauntered off.

I've been here ever since, and my back is aching. Could you hold this orb for a minute while I get some cushions?

Just for a sec, I swear!

JUPITER AND BAUCIS

READ THEIR STORY ON PAGES 28–29.

Fact file: JUPITER

JUPITER was the supreme god of the Romans, in charge of thunder, lightning, and storms. He and his wife, Juno, and his daughter, Minerva, formed a trio that watched over the Roman people.

Jupiter was extremely powerful, and he could throw thunderbolts down to earth to punish people who offended him. But although he was strict, he was usually fair. He enjoyed disguising himself, either as a mortal or an animal, and mixing with ordinary humans.

JUPITER IN HIS OWN WORDS:

WHY I'M THE BEST:
When I divided up the world with my brothers, Neptune got the oceans and Pluto got the Underworld, but I took the heavens – obviously the choicest kingdom!

CHECK OUT MY RIDE:
I have a beautiful winged horse called Pegasus.

FAVORITE HOBBY:
Going in disguise to see what the mortals get up to. Hey, somebody has to make sure they're worshipping me properly!

HOW TO MAKE ME ANGRY:
Show me any sort of disrespect, and you'll get a thunderbolt in a very painful place …

Fact file: BAUCIS

BAUCIS was a cheerful old peasant woman who lived with her husband, Philemon, in the region that is now Turkey. They had a simple cottage and a small farm, and although they were poor, they were deeply in love and very happy.

When they were granted a wish, Baucis and Philemon asked that they would die at the same time, so that neither would have to live without the other. And one day, when they were very old, they both sprouted leaves and turned into trees that grew entwined together.

BAUCIS IN HER OWN WORDS:

I COULDN'T LIVE WITHOUT:
My husband Philemon, the best thing that ever happened to me. We may not have a lot, but we have each other, and that's enough.

WORDS TO LIVE BY:
You can't turn away a guest!

IF I WON THE LOTTERY:
I guess I'd spruce the place up a bit, but nothing too fancy. I really don't need much.

UNEXPECTED GUESTS ... BAUCIS'S STORY

Everyone always asks how my husband and I came to be guardians of this temple. Sit yourself down and have a cup of tea, and I'll tell you how it happened.

Philemon and I were poor, and our cottage was small, but it was tidy and we were happy. One night there was a knock at the door. It was two tall handsome men, one young and one older. We didn't have much to spare, but of course I invited them in anyway.

I started preparing a meal and asked the two men if they had come far. "Very far," said the older one. "And every other door was closed in our faces."

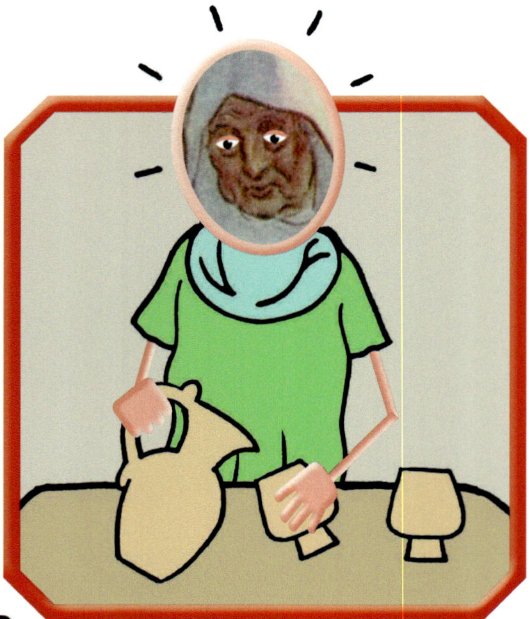

Well, it's true that some of our neighbors are not very friendly. I started to put out olives, cheese, and figs. Our guests didn't seem to mind how plain it was and chatted pleasantly with us while they ate.

I thought we might run out of wine, but every time I looked at the jug, it was still full – like magic. With a gasp, I realized what that meant and elbowed Philemon. "They must be gods!" I whispered.

He went pale and fell on his knees, arthritis and all. "Forgive us, lords, for how little we have to give you!"

I knew what we had to do. We had a pet goose, and if we killed it, it would make a meal fit for the gods. So I started chasing it around the room, and Philemon soon joined me. But we couldn't catch it, and the older man raised a hand to stop us. "Leave the goose alone," he said, "and follow us."

As we left the house, I could see clearly that our guests were Jupiter and Mercury. My knees were trembling, but I followed them to the top of a hill and looked back. The entire village had been flooded! Only our cottage was still above water, and as we watched it turned into a beautiful temple. "Your neighbors have been punished for turning us away," said Jupiter. "But in thanks for your hospitality, you will be the guardians of my new temple." And here we are today!

GLOSSARY

ANCESTOR a person from whom someone is descended, usually further back than a grandparent

ATONE to do something good to make up for a bad thing that you have done

BLACKSMITH a person who makes or repairs things made of iron or other metals

CHARIOT a carriage with two wheels that is pulled by horses. Chariots were used for racing as well as in battle.

CONSTELLATION a group of stars in the sky that seems to form a particular shape

DEMIGOD a person who is semi-divine, such as the child of a god and a mortal

DESCENDANT someone who is related to a particular person who lived long ago

EMPIRE a large area of land ruled by a single emperor

ETRUSCANS a group of people who lived in Italy before the time of the Romans

FORGE a blacksmith's workshop, where objects are made by heating and shaping metal

FOUND to set up a settlement or organization for the first time

IMMORTAL living forever and never dying or decaying. The gods and goddesses of ancient Rome were immortal.

MORTAL an ordinary person who will eventually die instead of living forever

MYCENAE a city-state in ancient Greece

MYTH a traditional story that tries to explain why the world is the way that it is, or to recount legendary events

NYMPH a nature spirit often pictured as a beautiful woman living in a river, forest, or other location

PYRE a large pile of wood or other fuel for burning a dead body

QUINTILIS a month in the Roman calendar

SACRIFICE to give a gift to the gods, such as food or slaughtered animals.

SPARTA a city-state in ancient Greece, famous for its fierce warriors

TEMPLE a building devoted to the worship of one or more gods

THUNDERBOLT an imaginary pointed missile that flies down to earth along with a lightning flash. The Romans believed that Jupiter could hurl thunderbolts as a punishment.

TITANS the older generation of Greek gods who were overthrown by Zeus and his siblings

TROJAN WAR a legendary war in which an army of Greeks attacked the city of Troy in order to take back Queen Helen, who had been kidnapped by a Trojan prince

BOOKS

The Romans (Britain in the Past), Moira Butterfield, Franklin Watts

Gory Gladiators, Savage Centurions and Caesar's Sticky End: a Menacing History of the Unruly Romans! (Awfully Ancient), Kay Barnham, Wayland

The Orchard Book of Roman Myths, Geraldine McCaughrean, Orchard Books

Roman Myths: Retold from the Classic Originals, Diane Namm, Sterling Publishing

WEBSITES

Go here to find out more about the main Roman gods and goddesses:
http://www.roman-empire.net/children/gods.html

Learn more about Castor and Pollux at:
https://www.astrosafe.co/article/castor_and_pollux

This website gives more information on the 12 tasks of Hercules:
http://www.perseus.tufts.edu/Herakles/labors.html

Note to parents and teachers: Every effort has been made by the Publishers to ensure that these websites are suitable for children, that they are of the highest educational value, and that they contain no inappropriate or offensive material. However, because of the nature of the internet, it is impossible to guarantee that the contents of these sites will not be altered. We strongly advise that internet access is supervised by a responsible adult.

INDEX